This Is
George Washington

Daniel Shepard

Rigby®

A Harcourt Achieve Imprint

www.Rigby.com
1-800-531-5015

This is George.

We see him
on a dollar bill.

This is George.

We see him
on a quarter.

This is George.

We see him
on a book.

This is George.

We see him
on a stamp.

This is George.

We see him
on a sign.

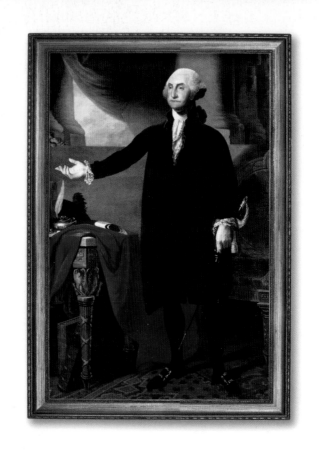

. This is George.

We see him
on a mountain.

This is George.

We see him
on a boat.

This is George Washington!